HOW TO TEXT MEN

Texts That Will Make Him Want You

Joshua Bell

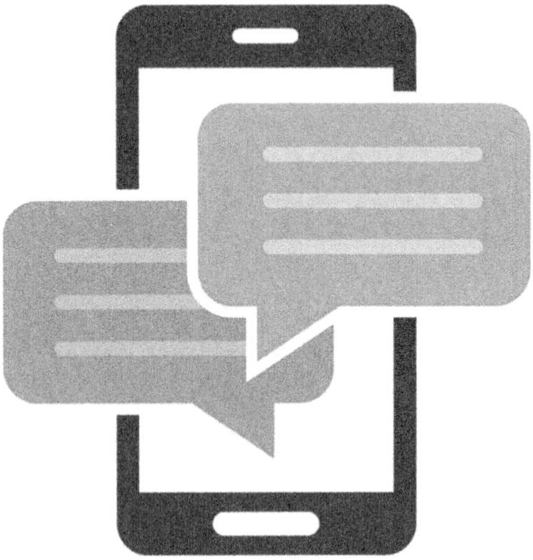

Published by *Monkey Publishing*

Edited by *Lily Marlene Booth*

Cover Design by *Diogo Lando*

Printed by *Amazon*

ISBN (Print): 978-1074724115

ASIN (eBook): B07SNGTDY4

1st Edition, published in 2019

© 2019 by Monkey Publishing

Monkey Publishing

Lerchenstrasse 111

22767 Hamburg

Germany

All rights reserved, including the right to reproduce this book or portions thereof in any form whatsoever except for brief quotations in critical reviews or articles, without the prior written permission of the publisher.

CONTENT

THE GOLDEN RULES OF TEXTING	9
Don't overlook your spelling.	11
Don't ever just say ´hey´.	13
Never Ever Drunk Text.	14
If you hit three, it's time to let it be.	15
Cut back on the emoji	15
Don't wait for him to make the first move.	17
Make him smile and laugh	19
Make plans and be specific	20
Be aware of your tone	22
Stop worrying about response times	23
Don't be a constant distraction	25
Stop with the questions	26
Be the real deal	27

LEARN HOW TO GRAB HIS ATTENTION... AND KEEP IT!	29
The Importance of Confidence	30
The Power of Positivity	31
Learn How to Make a First Impression Count	34
Don't look desperate.	37
Why a guy loves a damsel in distress	37
Learn to be funny	38
Seek out common interests	38

Thing you should NEVER text	41
HOW TO FLIRT THROUGH TEXT – LEARN TO DRIVE HIM WILD!	**45**
Learn the importance of being unique, and how to draw on your own experiences.	47
TEXTING IN A RELATIONSHIP	**52**
WHAT TEXTS DO GUYS WANT TO SEE?	**67**
How do guys change their texting habits if they like you?	68
5 Texts men actually want to receive	72
WHAT DO GUYS NOT WANT?	**Fehler! Textmarke nicht definiert.**
The Top 4 Turn Offs	89
Boring conversation	90
Texting Too Often	91
Not Texting Enough.	91
Vague Messages	92
Dismissing Their Compliments	93
Complaints about the 'Seen' Receipt	93
Compliment Fishing	94
Negging	94
RESOLVING CONFLICT THROUGH TEXT	**97**
The Basics	100
The RISC Technique	102
WHAT DO YOU DO WHEN IT DOESN'T WORK OUT?	**106**

How to know if he's playing games	107
What to do if he's losing interest.	117
Is it ever okay to break up through text?	123

INTRODUCTION

It won't surprise you when I say the cell phone has revolutionized the dating scene. Not since the invention of the automobile has a piece of technology had such an impact on human behavior. Whether you're in a relationship or not, the central focus of your interactions with other people will most likely be the cell phone. And although it can be used for a myriad of things, we often find ourselves texting more than anything else.

Texting is a super-fast, super-convenient way to talk to someone, especially if you're nervous about speaking to them face to face. Yet, as fantastic as texting is, it can often be a minefield of social etiquette. Have you ever been eager to text your crush, but as soon as your thumbs hit your phone you find yourself panicking about what to say? You might be wondering:

Should I text him first or should I wait for him?

What do I say?

If I reply too soon will I look desperate?

We've all been there and thought these things. Luckily, we're here to guide through the dos and don'ts of texting a guy. From essential rules you should always follow, ways to keep him engaged and what men actually want to see in a text, we've got you covered. So let's dive in and get started.

THE GOLDEN RULES OF TEXTING

Texting has become a communication revolution since the late 90's. From being a favorite of tech-savvy individuals, it has become an all-inclusive need of people and an extremely convenient means of social contact even further utilized to forge relationships including the romantic kind. Simply put, you can use texting as an innovative tool in flirting and dating.

When used properly and creatively, texting offers a great advantage in getting the person who piqued your interest. Its beauty lies in the opportunity of reconsidering what your response would be before tapping on the "Send" button. You can take your time to come up with a witty response and impress him with it. You don't even have to suffer the awkward silence or forced pleasantries that a phone call demands. However, there are drawbacks in using texting as a means to convey feelings towards a special person. Overdoing the use of emoticons, writing more than what's necessary, and lack of in-person communication are but a few to name.

Women must first take into consideration the psychology of the opposite sex. Men have a different perspective when it comes to texting. Females text to deepen bonds and relationships; men text to acquire information which is why they're big fans of brief and precise messages.

Catching the interest of your ideal guy means understanding his mindset. You can call this a part of your strategy and it may be the most crucial one.

It may mean going against your instincts or desires but understand that if you want to make your goals work, then you have to play by the rules.

This chapter will guide you through the do's and don'ts of texting with the aim of getting your ideal man get interested in you.

Don't overlook your spelling.

We know paying attention to grammar and worrying about correct spelling isn't sexy, but it is essential. Not only will you look as though you've thoroughly thought about your message before you sent it, but it ensures you don't look like a kid. Think of it this way. Which of these texts looks as though it came from someone who would be fun and interesting to chat to?

Hey bae u up 4 meeting ltr?

Or,

Hi, I was just wondering if you're free tonight to meet up for a drink. Would be great to see you.

Clarity in communication is vital when you're trying to get a guy's attention. Research conducted by Dr Eric Klinenberg along with comedian Aziz Ansari, discovered that with each and every one of their participants, bad spelling was seen as a sure-fire way to not be attracted to someone. Mainly, this is because a text message with abbreviations such as plz, bae, hun, l8r etc... made the person they were speaking to appear lazy, disinterested and unintelligent.

This may seem harsh, after all, good spelling isn't everyone's strong point. However, you can make sure you don't make obvious mistakes. Showing that you're paying attention to how your text is constructed, shows you're paying attention to your crush.

But it isn't just spelling. Research conducted at Binghamton University showed how the use of a full stop influenced how you're viewed by the person you're texting. Research participants were shown a series of texts, some with periods at the end of the sentences, some without. It was discovered that the texts that ended with periods were viewed as less sincere. Meanwhile, messages that ended with an exclamation point were viewed as more sincere! This may seem peculiar, but think of it this way. If you asked someone out on a date, which one these replies seems the most genuine?

I'd love to.

Or,

I'd love to!

But why is this? Generally, it is assumed the use of a period at the end of a sentence conveys a finality to the discussion. It's seen as more formal, less relaxed and appears as though the conversation is drawing to a close.

Don't ever just say ´hey´.

It can be tempting just to send the odd message saying hi/hello/hey. After all, isn't that how you start a conversation? It may seem logical in real life, however, it comes across as deeply unattractive in the texting world. Let's look a little deeper as to why that is. Once again, Ansari and Klinenberg teamed up to research what participants thought of receiving a text message with the single word 'hey'.

The results showed that every single one of the participants agreed that 'hey' was not what they wanted to hear. But how can a word that's so harmless be so off putting to your crush? Put simply, it's because it's generic and lazy. It makes the recipient believe you're not making an effort in wanting to speak to them. And because of its simplicity, it gives the impression you probably send out a dozen 'heys' every day.

Furthermore, there is nothing in a text of this nature that suggests you want to have a conversation. There's no information about how you feel or how your crush is. Even a message such as, *Hey, how's it going?* Is miles more enticing as it shows that you want to know how they are and you're interested in them.

But that's not it. A generic 'hey' is just about the easiest message to ignore. It's not asking for anything and it's certainly not giving anything. It's just boring and unfeeling, and if your texts come across that way, chances are you do too.

Wow. Who knew 'hey' could be so bad?

Never Ever Drunk Text.

Ever! This is something we all know we shouldn't do but most of us have done at some point. But there's nothing more annoying than hearing your phone beep in the middle of the night and seeing you've received a drunken text full of gibberish. If the shoe was on the other foot, would you want that? Chances are you might not.

Most of the time, sending a guy a drunk text is a definite way to turn him right off you. But apart from the obvious reasons, why is this?

Firstly, it's because it shows you have little self-control. As we all know, we're far more likely to say and do things after a few drinks than when we're sober. So chances are you'll regret sending that message at three in the morning that made perfect sense at the time but makes you cringe when you wake up.

Secondly, texting a guy when you're drunk eliminates the chance for him to get a little jealous.

If he knows you're out, he might worry other guys are hitting on you, and this is a good thing! It keeps him interested. Nothing increases a guy's desire for you than knowing there's a chance he might not be able to have you.

Thirdly, it looks desperate as hell. And nothing screams more desperate than demanding to speak to someone when you're drunk.

If you hit three, it's time to let it be.

There's an unspoken rule in the texting world that if you text someone three times and don't get a response, you just have to accept they're not interested. It sounds harsh, but accepting this will save a lot of heartache in the long run. If a person doesn't text back once, it's not likely to be a big deal. They could be busy or unable to get to their phone. If they don't text back twice, you should maybe take it as a warning. It could just be a coincidence and once again they could be too busy to answer you. But if they ignore your third text it's time to call it quits. Being ignored three times in a row is a message in itself.

Cut back on the emoji

I'm a little partial to the occasional emoji. Who doesn't like getting a smiley cat face? But there's a difference between sending a smiley face every now and again and bombarding someone with poop and peach emoji. A recent survey by dating app, Plenty of Fish revealed the three emoji that are least likely to get a response from people is the eggplant, the peach and the fire emoji. That's hardly surprising. After all, we know getting sent the eggplant isn't a hint to get more vegetables in our diet.

But the sleaziness of certain emoji isn't the only reason they're a turnoff for guys. They're also immature, and when a guy looks at his phone and sees a long row of pink hearts he thinks he's texting a school kid, which, believe me, is not what he wants. Not to mention emoji can sometimes send out the wrong signals. A red devil, for example, is sexy to some people, but might just be plain weird or appear angry to others.

They're also impersonal and lack the warmth and feeling that human interaction relies on. If you have a feeling you want to communicate, there's no doubt it will be received and understood better if you actually say it with words. Furthermore, they don't actually add anything to a conversation. If anything they're an annoying distraction.

But if you really can't send a message without reaching that thumb for the emoji then make sure to tone it down. According to Plenty of Fish, there is at least a couple emoji that aren't completely despised; the winking smiley face and the heart eyes smiley. Just make sure not to send ten of them in a row.

Don't wait for him to make the first move.

You're a modern woman and can do whatever you want, including texting that guy in the office you always found cute. That doesn't mean you should come on strong and appear desperate. It just means you don't have to sit around waiting for him to text you until you go gray. If you want to text your crush, go for it. There's nothing stopping you.

For years there has been a myth that if a woman makes the first move, she makes a bad impression, but that's simply not the case. A guy won't think badly of you for texting him first. If anything, he'll be flattered and think you're a strong-minded woman who knows what she wants. Which is always attractive! And if he does think any less of you just because you made the first move, you're better off without him!

Relationships expert Harris O'Malley suggests we should get in touch with our crush as soon as possible, because if we don't, two things might happen. He might think you're not interested in him, or worse, he might just forget about you. It's better to text him within a day so you're keeping things moving and building up the excitement and momentum.

There's no need to worry about them not being attracted to you at this point. I mean, they already gave you their number so they must like you, right? So don't worry about it looking as though you're coming on too strong. He'll more than likely be excited to hear from you.

Showing and conveying your interest shows confidence. It isn't a crime to be the first one to say, "Hi!" to the guy you like nor does it degrade your value as a woman. Even cyber-dating experts agree that women who show assertiveness attract guys better.

If you're texting him for the first time after your first meeting, try fun and catchy lines that can make his heart flutter. For instance, you can tell him something like, "Last night left me thinking about you," or "I really enjoyed yesterday. Looking forward to the next time <insert winking emoji>."

Now if you just met him online via dating app, compliment his profile picture or make it a pivotal point to start a conversation. A witty but sincere opener will definitely get you a reply. Try something like these lines:

- "That's a dazzling smile you've got. I almost melted right in my seat."
- "That's a nice profile photo. I also have fun memories of Barcelona last month <insert smiley with blushing cheeks>."
- "You remind me of my favorite coffee: tall, dark, strong, and energizing."

Mundane lines like "What's up?" or "Hey, handsome/hottie!" might get you a response but won't get you a deep, lasting impression. A bold, confident woman with humor gets a guy hooked.

You're already a grown woman who should know what she wants and can effectively articulate it. Cut the girlish uncertainties like "There will be a party tonight. I heard that Zayn Malik of 1D will perform there. You should come. Everyone's gonna be there," or "What are your plans for the weekend? I heard that it's going to be sunny. My friends were wondering if you can join us since we're going to the beach." You don't need to elaborate on everything and make your friends your dummy or excuse. Keep in mind that you're no longer a timid, gawky high schooler but an assertive, mature woman who will get straight to the point about what she wants. Instead of wordy text messages that go in circles, opt for no-nonsense assertions. Say, "Let's go to the party tonight. I'm sure we'll both enjoy it!" or "Hey, my friends and I are going to the beach. You should join us."

Make him smile and laugh

Generally, people like those who can make them smile and laugh. Men are no exception. When we smile or laugh, we feel positive energies flowing everywhere, both inside and outside us. And when we feel positively energized, we believe that we can do anything! This is the reason why we tend to like (or love) those who can make us laugh and smile.

For you who want to impress your ideal guy, the idea might be a little bit daunting since humor depends on how a person perceives it to be. However, there are still tricks that can surely work on him.

First, call him by his name. This creates intimacy helping you draw closer to him and him to you. It reminds him of his importance as an individual, boosting his self-esteem and — of course — his attention to you.

Second, compliment him. Go for spicy but harmless pick-up lines that could boost a little of his ego. This can help you get closer to him.

Make plans and be specific

Now that you got things moving, you need to keep things rolling. You're chatting now, so that means he's likely to be interested. So don't just sit around texting about vague things and not actually meeting up. Set a date and see each other face to face.

There are numerous reasons why you should make plans to meet up sooner rather than later.

First, the constant back and forth of text messages, although helping you bond at a mental level, is doing nothing to ignite the physical spark. It can also create the peculiar phenomenon where you've created an entire virtual persona for the guy, and by the time you meet in real life, you find your expectations haven't been met.

One relationships expert, Emily Morse calls this premature escalation due to people building up a mental picture of someone through what they are being told via text messages, only to discover the reality is much different.

So how do you text to make plans? Make sure to keep things specific. A message such as, *Hey, wanna hang out sometime?* Appears keen and friendly, but it won't elicit the excitement and commitment you're after. You need to solidify a plan so you make that first date happen. Instead, focus on actual things that you can do together. For example,

Hi, do you fancy grabbing a bite to eat Friday night? Or *Wanna go see a movie with me tonight?* is far more likely to get the response you want.

Remember this, your texts should be a build up to an event such as a date. Not the event itself.

Be aware of your tone

Often, what we think in our heads or say out loud doesn't translate well in a text. Texting is a fantastic way to speak to someone, but one of its flaws is that it makes it difficult to figure out someone's tone of voice. This means you need to be careful if you're flirting, joking or being sarcastic. What's funny to you might come across as rude to the other person or your well intended sarcasm might be taken seriously.

This may mean that you have to be conscious of your punctuation, capitalization, spelling, and use of words. Read the following messages:

- "WHERE R U NOW?" (Sounds like a demand even if you're only asking about his location at the moment.)
- "Okay, let's go" (Lack of exclamation mark may sound you're not excited at all.)
- "I don't care!" (Angry tone, put a period if you simply mean that you don't mind something.)

You don't want to sound bossy, condescending, bitter, too formal or calculating. Always keep your tone positive, polite, and sweet since you're still in the trying-to-impress-him stage— that's only natural.

There's nothing wrong in toning down your messages when you believe they come on too strong. The best way to determine this is to read your messages loud enough for your ears. The way you read them should give you the idea of how the text recipient would take it. If you're not too sure about your tone, try to tone it down using a proper emoticon.

One way you can stop yourself accidentally sending a text that can be interpreted the wrong way is to pause before you send, re-read it and imagine how someone might interpret it if they didn't know you. Would your flirty joke appear creepy and weird? Would your sarcasm just look like passive aggression? If the answer is yes then rethink how you're communicating what you're trying to say. And if you're still in doubt, read the text out loud.

However, you can make things simple by thinking about it this way. Don't text something that you wouldn't say to the person in real life.

Stop worrying about response times

I know it's frustrating when you see someone has read your message, but they haven't replied. Your brain is jumping to conclusions at the speed of light thinking all sorts of terrible things. *Did I say something wrong? Do they not like me? Are they playing mind games?*

There isn't a simple answer to make you stop worrying. You can, however, keep it cool and try not to think too hard about why someone hasn't texted you back. There could be a hundred reasons why that don't even have anything to do with you.

But what about how long you should wait before replying? If you look online and in relationship books, there appears to be a whole host of magic formulas and theories about how long you should wait before texting back. Some people say you should wait exactly three minutes, while others say you should wait twice as long as the other person before firing back a text.

Personally, I think all of that is nonsense. If you want to reply to someone, then reply. It's as simple as that. Mind games lead to nothing but a sore head, so do what you want.

Besides, once you get to know the person and you're talking regularly, you'll fall into a texting rhythm and you won't have to think about the mysterious response time any more.

But I don't want to look desperate by texting back right away! I hear you scream. *Surely if play hard to get I'll appear more attractive?*

So here's the thing. There has been research conducted that shows if you make someone wait for your reply, you're more likely to seem attractive, desirable, and hard to get. And men love the chase, right? But the problem is, this only works in the short term, and in the long run, you're just going to look as though you're manipulative and playing games. And that's never a good look.

Don't be a constant distraction

One of the best tricks in keeping a guy interested in you via text messaging? Learn to respect his time and space. Don't text him while he's at work, doing something important — it's that simple. He's not going to devote time and effort to send you messages to initiate a conversation when he should actually be doing his job. This alone can fetch you a lot of brownie points.

Keeping your text messages when you know he's busy shows that you respect his commitments and the importance of his work. Reserve your text messages for lunchtime or break time. During these times, you can send him sweet texts that can help boost his energy levels and make him smile. Let us give you some examples:

"Using this time to tell you how much I miss you..."

"Hope you're having a great day and hope this message can make it even better."

Send him a picture of a cupcake (or anything sweet) with this caption: "Nothing sweeter than your smile."

"I wish I could be your computer monitor... So I can be closer to you."

Stop with the questions

You're having a conversation and trying to get to know the guy but this doesn't mean you work for the FBI. One of the biggest turnoffs for a guy is being bombarded with a hundred and one questions. I mean, it's great to ask questions, that's how a conversation works. You say a little bit about yourself then ask about the other person so they can respond. A good conversation should be like a ping pong match and be balanced and reciprocal.

However, asking too making questions before the guy has even had a chance to respond to the first one probably makes it look as though you're not really listening. And it also makes him feel as though he's under attack and being interrogated. Meanwhile, the constant focus on him might make him think you don't have anything to contribute to the conversation about yourself.

Try and learn how to mix in statements and info about yourself in with the questions so the conversation flows easier and has more balance. For example, instead of

Where are you going on holiday this year? You got plans this summer? You ever been to Hawaii?

Say this instead:

Have you made plans for the summer yet? I'm thinking of visiting Hawaii this year.

You can also learn to use open ended questions which give the conversation a more 'flowy' easy breezy feel rather than it feeling like a formal interview. Open questions are questions that you can't answer with a yes or no. So for example instead of texting:

Did you like the movie?

You could say,

What did you think about the movie?

It's a subtle, barely perceivable change, but it makes a huge impact on your conversation. Firstly, it eliminates his ability to just give a one word answer. Secondly, it encourages him to talk about himself and his thoughts and feelings toward the movie, and will therefore make you appear more interested in him.

Be the real deal

Despite the pressure the challenge demands from you plus the rules you have to observe, there's nothing better than staying true and sincere. Be your authentic self. You may get a perfect score by following the texting etiquette but if you're insincere, lying, and creating a totally different person, then you're nothing but a sham.

What truly makes a woman beautiful is her honesty and confidence, so be sure to have these two qualities. So if he gives you the cold shoulder upon knowing your true self, there are only two reasons for that: He's not into you and obviously, he's not the right one for you.

On the flip side, think about what would happen if he falls in love with your pseudo persona and wants to take your texting relationship further. You go on dates and as you spend time together, he realizes that you're not the same woman he fell in love with. How do you think he would react? Obviously, he will feel cheated. What's more... the ugly truth about relationships built on lies is that they always fall apart. Wanting to achieve your goal doesn't give you the license to deceive somebody.

LEARN HOW TO GRAB HIS ATTENTION...AND KEEP IT!

Okay, now you have a handle on the basics of texting. So let's put it all into practice! Now that you know what to do and what not do, you can begin to start thinking about how you're gonna grab your crush's attention and more importantly, how you're gonna keep him hanging on your every word. But before you dive right in and send that text, take some time to think about what guys are attracted to, and what's going to grab his attention right away.

The Importance of Confidence

Nothing makes you more attractive than having confidence. That doesn't necessarily mean you have to show off and strut around looking like a million dollars, but it does mean you have to be comfortable with yourself. Whether you're an Instagram model, an emo or a bookworm, own your personality! No one can be quite like you and all the things that make you unique are what make you attractive. Don't shy away from your quirks because they're what make you fabulous and stand out from the crowd.

But I know it's not always possible to feel that inner confidence. Sometimes it's all too easy to fall into the trap of low self-esteem. I know, I've been there too. So how do you bring out that confidence? Well, first of all, don't worry too much about looks. They're not everything and you are a whole package with so much more to offer than what you look like.

Inner confidence comes from truly loving yourself and knowing your self-worth.

If you're having a tough time learning to love yourself, focus on all the positive things in your life, such as what you're good at. Nothing boosts self-esteem more than knowing you're the best at something, whether that be rustling up a delicious dinner, killing it on the dance floor, or running a mile in under ten minutes. Whatever it is, focus on it and fully appreciate just how awesome you are. You'll be feeling that confidence in no time and in turn, that inner love and appreciation for yourself will beam right out of you. No one will be able to ignore it. Including your crush.

Believe in yourself, know how incredible you are and he won't be able to stay away.

The Power of Positivity

Nothing is less attractive than negativity. Not only will it make you feel bad, but it will make everyone around you utterly miserable. But most importantly, positivity is a contagious state. So if you're having a good day, so will everyone in your orbit, including that guy you want to notice you. Maya Angelou, one of the world's greatest writers, once said, "I've learned that people will forget what you said, people will forget what you did, but people will never forget how you made them feel."

If you let yourself become clouded by negative thoughts it will come through in your actions and how you interact with people. Not only will this make you not fun to be around, but it will also make you isolated and even more miserable.

While a bad day can sometimes overwhelm our emotions and make us want to talk about it for the sake of letting go, it won't be a wise idea to share it with your crush. Save this kind of talk for your best friend. Remember that you're still in an early stage where creating impressions do matter. You don't want him getting the idea that you're a negative person, do you?

Don't send him texts relating to work issues and your frustrations. Put yourself in his shoes. What if you received a text saying, "My boss dumped all his work on me," I'm the one doing his job but he's the one reaping all the rewards! What an ass!" Awkward isn't it? Although it will be a totally different tale if you two are in a steady relationship until then, resist the urge.

Little complaints won't do any good either, especially when you word them heavily. For example: "Had a crazy morning! I couldn't remember where I put my car keys so I had to take the bus and I'm in heels BTW. Gosh, promise, I felt my makeup melting in this heat!" You would sound like a spoiled, whiny high school girl who cannot handle life's little challenges.

On the other hand, it would have been a lot different if you put it in a lighter way. It would probably be something like this:

- Guy: How's ur morning?
- You: A bit crazy but manageable.
- Guy: How?
- You: Well, I had to take the bus since I misplaced my car keys.
- Guy: That's "crazy" for you?
- You: When you have to be in your 7-inch heels, running in this heat not to be late. Wait… I should say, I look cool there.

Of course, being positive all the time is easier said than done. We all have bad days. Hell, some of us have entire bad months or years. That doesn't mean you can't try to infuse each day with a little positive thinking to make the best of things.

Keeping an upbeat outlook will change your life. Start thinking positive things and you will see the best in every situation. However, if you're having difficulty focusing on the positive things in your life, try this little exercise. Every night before bed, write down three things that happened during the day that you are grateful for. They don't have to be big things and can be anything from a great cup of coffee you had to a new book you bought or a hug from a friend. As long as it's positive, it's doing the job.

This exercise might seem insignificant, but its impact is huge. Research conducted within the behavioural psychology field has shown that performing this task for twenty-one days can rewire your brain to see more positive things in your life. In essence, this means if you note down how appreciative you are for all the good things in your life, your brain will go looking for other things to be grateful for. Pretty cool, right?

So how does this help you grab the attention of your crush? Well, there's nothing sexier than a happy person who's shining with positive vibes. Start thinking positively and he'll be attracted to you like a moth to a flame in no time!

Learn How to Make a First Impression Count

Okay, so you have your eyes on your crush and you've got his attention with all that positivity and self-confidence that's shining out of you. Now how do you keep his attention?

This sounds scarier than it actually is. Chances are you're overthinking things and worrying about a bunch of stuff he hasn't even noticed. The key is to be friendly and polite, not coming across as too arrogant or too shy while keeping his attention. If this sounds a bit overwhelming, don't worry because we've got a few tips and tricks to help you make the best first impression.

1. Actually listen to him. I know, you're nervous so you're probably fumbling your words, but asking him the same question twice by mistake will make you look as though you're disinterested in what he has to say. Take things slow and really listen to what he's saying. Don't feel under pressure to speak and rush through a conversation. Just chill and let it come naturally.

2. Stop talking about yourself. If you find yourself babbling about yourself because you're either nervous or you've run out of things to say, take a step back and ask him questions about himself. Not only will this make you look even more interested in him, but it will give you the chance to take a break and let him lead the conversation.

3. Make eye contact. Fun fact: If someone looks deep into your eyes for longer than three seconds the first time you meet, they have already decided if they want to f**k you or fight you. That may surprise you, but it all comes down to our primal, evolutionary instincts. We make snap judgements about people to ascertain if they are safe or a danger, friend or foe.

But if you find your crush staring into your eyes for longer than three seconds, it's doubtful he wants to fight you. Not unless you made a really bad first impression. Hopefully he'll be thinking the same thing you are and is communicating his attraction to you by gazing into your eyes. But primal instincts aside, staring into his eyes will give a clear signal that you're interested. Just make sure to not do it for too long or you'll look a little creepy.

4. Use his name. Having him hear you say his name will make him feel special. Pair this with making eye contact and he'll be hearing your message loud and clear. You don't have to start every sentence with his name, but dropping it into conversation once or twice will let him know your attention is all on him.

5. Try to avoid awkward silences. We've all been there. You're chatting away and then suddenly there's nothing but an eerie silence and there may as well be crickets chirping in the background. But awkward silences are more than just a little embarrassing. They also make you look as though you don't want to talk to him. At worst, they make you appear boring with nothing to say.

So make sure to fill that lull in conversation with a few words. They don't have to be poignant or super deep. A light-hearted comment or a joke will do wonders to keep the conversation going. Just make sure you shy away from saying something that's even more boring than the silence. Nothing is more awkward than having to make small talk about the weather.

Okay, so you're super confident, full of positivity, and you've made a killer first impression. Now what? Here, we have a look at some extra tips that can really help you keep his attention.

Don't look desperate.

I know, you've now got that guy to talk to you and you're really eager to get him to like you, but trying too hard is more likely to push him away. You need to draw a fine line between him knowing you like him, and feeling suffocated by you. The last thing he wants is to feel as though you're bombarding him with attention and he can't breathe.

Try not to act insecure and definitely don't be possessive. If you're worried that you might appear desperate, you can ask your friends to keep you in check. This way you can learn to take a step back and give him some space. They'll be able to see things in your behavior that you might not notice.

Why a guy loves a damsel in distress

There's something hard-wired into a guy's brain where he just can't resist a damsel in distress. Countless romantic comedies have a scene where a woman drops something and the guy rushes to her aid only for the romance of the century to occur. I'm not saying you should pretend to faint when he walks by. But you could maybe ask him to help you carry your bags. If you're worried this may sound like an imposition, don't. Humans are built to be helpful creatures. It's what has helped our survival for thousands of years. People love to help others. Especially guys. Once your bags are in his hands, he's all yours. Make sure to show how grateful you are with a big smile.

Learn to be funny

Don't worry, you don't have to craft your own stand up show, but being silly and goofy and not taking yourself seriously makes you more attractive than you realize. If you can make a guy laugh, you've got his attention. Learn to laugh at yourself and he'll see that you're not fixated on your ego. Believe me, if you can make a crush laugh, you'll be keeping his attention.

Seek out common interests

This is essential because if you find an activity that you both like doing, then you're on the fast track to a first date. Not only that, but you've got an excuse to text him! Remember, shared interests don't always have to be shared hobbies, they can also be a love for the same music, a shared religion or sharing similar moral values.

Okay, so now you've gotten his attention long enough to get his number. You've shown him how confident you are, made your thoughts crystal clear with some sexy eye contact, sought out common ground and made him chuckle. Now it's time to text.

But what do you say? It's more than likely you're feeling a little awkward about what to say to him. Do you tell him you had a great time with him? Do you randomly send him a sexy joke? Or do you dive right in and ask him out on a date? First, learn to chill and try not to worry too much. I got you. So let's take a look at some examples of things you can say to keep his interest sparked.

1. *You looked good in that shirt/hat/sweatshirt etc...* If you want to make a good impression with a first text, nothing will make him feel better than a compliment. Not only will it give his ego a boost but it will confirm that you're still interested in him. Reaching out with a compliment is a sure fire way to let him know what you feel, and he'll have no choice but to respond.

2. *Send memes.* I know, this may seem silly, but memes are extraordinary creations that not only make us laugh, but also bond us. Sending him a meme that's relevant to him will show that you're not only thinking about him, but that you've got a sense of humour and are eager to keep things light and entertaining.

3. *Text about something relevant.* If you're at school together you could text something like:

Hey, you get that essay finished?

Or if you work together you could text about a project or a meeting. Just find something relevant that you share and you'll have a conversation flowing in no time. More than likely, you'll end up starting to text about homework and the next thing you know you're chatting away about all sorts of things.

4. *I'm just about to grab lunch at -insert his favourite place- you wanna come along?* First, find me a guy that can turn down food. Or a woman for that matter. Second, dropping his favourite place into the text means he's more likely to want to come with you. Third, the immediacy of the message gives him less time to ponder his response. It's not like he has to think about it happening later on in the week and make plans. Lastly, the casual nature of asking him out this way will keep things light, and fun, and eliminates the pressure that you'd face on a formal date.

5. *I had the weirdest dream last night and you were in it.* Okay, this can go two ways. It might go down the path of a sexy dream, or it could just be something silly and funny. Either way, you will have piqued his curiosity and he'll be eager to know what you dreamed about. The magic of this text message is that you can steer the conversation any way you

want. Want to make it a little naughty? You can, but there's always the option of keeping things safe and savoury if you want to.

So now you have some amazing first texts you can fire at him, but is there anything you can't send? In short, yes. Let's go over them now.

Thing you should NEVER text

1. Nudes.

This is seen as a sure fire way to get someone's attention, but it isn't always the most sensible. There are many reasons as to why you shouldn't text your crush a nude photo. They can get leaked, they could jeopordize your future, (unless you've got your sights on being the next Kim Kardashian) and you may find that you've started something you're not comfortable with. One nude photo might not be enough and before long, you might feel yourself pressured to send more and more.

The most important thing to consider is your own comfort level. Don't ever let a guy pressure you into thinking you have to text nude photos to get his attention. If you don't want to do it, then don't. And if he makes you think you're not worth his attention because you won't send them, then you simply don't need him.

However, I'm sure there are some of you out there who are comfortable with sending nudes and if you are, then by all means don't feel as though you shouldn't. But don't send them right away. Make him wait! And always remember, you are worth more than just your looks and your nudity.

2. Big fat lies.

Sure, telling him you're an Olympic medalist and a part time Victoria's Secret model will make him want you, but sooner or later he's going to find out the truth and then what? Are you going to carry on lying to cover your tracks? Or are you going to come clean? Either way you're going to look both stupid and crazy and he won't want anything to do with you. There's nothing attractive about lying and there's nothing worse than being caught out. As tempting as it is to embellish the truth to appear more attractive, just don't.

3. Too many texts.

I know you just want to make sure he's talking to you, but sending one text right after the other looks desperate and he'll be overwhelmed. If you have something to say, send it as a well thought out, single message, don't just fire away one text after the other in a stream of consciousness.

4. The dreaded three scrollers.

You know the ones. You open your phone and see a wall of text that reads like a novel and takes you five minutes to get get through. Sending long messages that are more like short stories than texts will put him off, especially when you haven't really got to know each other yet.

By all means, if you have known each other a while and are in the habit of sending long messages, then don't stop. But if you've just met your crush and you're trying to make a good impression, sending these long, scrolling texts will make him feel like it's a chore to talk to you. You don't want him to be bored. You want to keep him eager so he wants to know more. Keep your texts short and sweet and that way he's more likely to be sweet on you.

5. Fake texts. Ever done this?

Hey, you still cool for later?

Oops, that wasn't meant for you! But how's it going?

You may be tempted to find an excuse to talk to your crush and some of us are guilty of texting them by 'mistake' just to get their attention. But your crush probably isn't stupid and the fact is that he'll no doubt sense you've faked it. Not to mention the conversation won't be organic. A false start will only create a false conversation. You're better off not playing around and actually texting him.

6. *Gossip.*

I don't mean the silly celebrity gossip that piques our attention at one time or another. I mean idle, bitchy gossip about someone you know. Although gossip is a part of life for most people, (in fact women are so used to bonding over gossip that they even produce the 'love' chemical Oxycotin when they do it) it doesn't mean it's attractive to a guy. Texting him with some little tidbit about a woman you hate will make you look petty, nasty and immature. Which is never a good look. Try and engage him in meaningful conversation instead which will not only help you get to know each other better, but will last longer.

7. Demands for a response.

This is the worst. It looks needy and possessive and will send him running for the hills. If a guy hasn't texted back don't pester him. There could be a hundred reasons why he hasn't responded and he shouldn't feel pressured to give you an explanation.

Maybe he was ill, maybe he was busy at work. Perhaps he just fell asleep. It's no big deal if he doesn't reply. Just chill and get on with your own life. He's more likely to text you back when he sees how much fun you're having without him.

HOW TO FLIRT THROUGH TEXT – LEARN TO DRIVE HIM WILD!

F lirting! I can hear you panic. *I can't do that! I'm not confident enough. What if I make a fool of myself? How do I even know what to do?*

For some lucky people, flirting comes as naturally as breathing. Yet for some of us it can make our minds go blank and give us sweaty palms. But it's okay, because I'll see you through the flirting process with some handy, easy to use techniques that will make it feel effortless.

What's also great about these techniques is that they can be implemented through text message so it takes away the stress involved with having to do it face to face.

So let's get started and soon he won't be able to resist you.

First, the key to flirting successfully via text message is to be witty, engaging, charming and sexy, all in just a couple sentences. Sounds intimidating, right? Well, it doesn't have to be. Not when there are certain rules you can follow. These are simple, fail-proof, and unbelievably effective. Let's go!

Learn the importance of being unique, and how to draw on your own experiences.

One of the things that make you most attractive is your uniqueness, but how do you convey that quickly through a text message? It's not like you can spell out your life story and give him a run down of all your specific quirks. What you can do, however, is draw on your own personal experiences and values to create texts that only you would write.

This could be a way to communicate your own special type of humour or insight into life. Leave him reading your messages thinking not a single other woman in the world can text like you can.

Be a tease.

No, I don't mean play games with him to make him lust after you only to get cold water thrown over his desires. I mean make fun of him in a cute, silly way. Be playful, show that you don't take yourself seriously and that he can tease you too. It's not about bullying each other and making mean comments, it's about being light-hearted and showing your humorous side. Letting him tease you and teasing him in return will show that you're not hung up on what people think about you and that you're not driven by your ego.

They key to making fun of him is to make sure he knows you're not being serious. Strangely enough, teasing, in a cute flirty way, comes across as a sign that you like someone. Not a sign that you're being nasty. This is because it comes across as shy and endearing, as though you're hiding your real, loving intentions behind a joke and a teasy text. He'll think you're cute, believe me.

Always leave him wanting more.

If you're trying to flirt rather than have a meaningful conversation, it may benefit you to play it cool. If you're trying to lure him in and keep his attention, be the first to leave a conversation. This doesn't mean simply ignoring him, which can come across as rude. But just saying you have to go or can't text anymore, will leave him wanting more.

This works because you're not dragging things out and wracking your brain for something new to say. This will only lead to boring chat. Instead, when you reach the point where he is most interested in you, sign off and tell him you'll get back to him later. He'll be disappointed, but in a good way, and he won't be able to stop thinking about talking to you again.

To amp things up, tell him you can't wait to speak to him again and it'll make him even more excited. The key here is to really escalate the anticipation of hearing from you.

Examples you can send include:

I gotta go meet my girls now. Can't wait to talk later.

Have to get back to work, but can't wait to chat later!

Got homework to finish. Chat tomorrow? :)

Gotta catch my beauty sleep. Text me in the morning?

Play truth or dare.

What is so fun about this is that you can have full control over the conversation and make things as dirty, silly, emotional, or safe as you want. It's also one of the most effective ways to flirt with a guy!

First, truth questions will help you bond, especially if you are asking personal questions. Furthermore, they can be something you can talk more about in person. Maybe even on a first date.

They can also be used as tools to learn more about your crush in a playful, less obvious way. It's definitely easier than just coming right out with an awkward question. In turn, it's a way for him to learn more about you.

Here are a few flirty truth questions to get your started:

What's the most embarrassing thing you've ever done?

Have you ever kissed someone you shouldn't?

Would you ever kiss me?

Meanwhile flirty dares can be as small or outrageous as you want them to be. They can be sexy, silly, crazy or tiny. It's up to you. Just make sure you don't feel pressured into doing something you don't want to.

Texts that give him no option but to ask you out.

Done properly, texting something innocuous can lead him to ask you out. That is if you lead him to… The key is to guide the conversation toward a date without looking as though you are. There are various ways you can do this. You can draw on the damsel in distress image so he feels compelled to meet you. Or you can draw on inspiration from playing truth or dare. What's important is that you don't come across as manipulative and that your message reads as though you actually want to see him, not that you're just playing games.

Examples of great messages to get him to ask you out look like this:

At a terrible house party. Can't take it anymore! Save me?

What would you rather do, A hundred push-ups or hang out with me?

I have to go to a boring family dinner tonight. I would literally rather do anything than go...

If you put this all together, flirting through text should be a breeze. What I personally love about flirting this way is that is relieves the pressure and anxiety of doing it face to face. And playing games such as truth or dare can really open a range of possibilities to learn about each other. It's an incredible way to bring out each other's personalities. Just ensure you don't take it too seriously.

TEXTING IN A RELATIONSHIP

So he's gone from your crush to your boyfriend and you're beginning the rollercoaster ride of the first few months of your relationship. Meeting someone and forming a relationship with them is probably the most exciting time of our lives. And nowadays, we have our cell phones by our side to makes things even easier!

It wasn't that long ago that people could only communicate by landline and you had to fight all your siblings to get the use of it. Even then, everyone in the house could hear you and it was only those who were very lucky who could have their own phone line in their room. And if you didn't have that, you were left with actual love letters sent the old fashioned way. And they could take days to arrive!

Thankfully, now we can send anything from a thought, a line of poetry, a cat meme or a video in a matter of seconds. So take advantage of it and use your cell phone to help build your relationship. As you enter a new phase with your boyfriend as you become officially a couple, you may find that your texting habits change as you become closer. This may have you wondering what to do. Is this the time when you start coming up with a nickname? Do you text him less now that you're together? Or more?

Don't fret. Let me guide you through the ins and outs of relationship texting. I've compiled the best texting tips and tricks that will help solidify your relationship in those rocky early weeks and months.

Why you should start the day with a morning text.

Is there anything better than waking up to a text from someone you're in love with. I've heard countless times from women that it just makes their heart jump to know a guy's been thinking about them as soon as he's woken up. Well, it's no different for guys. Sending a quick text to say good morning will brighten his day and let him know you were thinking about him too, and maybe even dreaming about him...

Stop over analyzing.

In the early days of a relationship, when you're still getting to know each other, it's easy to read every word of their message looking for nuances and hidden meanings that aren't really there.

Why did he put two Xs at the end of this message when he put three yesterday? What did he mean by see ya later? Does that mean he actually wants to see me later? Or was it just a turn of phrase?

Worrying too much when he doesn't text back immediately or what he means by a simple "yep" doesn't help you at all! If you give an equally drastic reaction such as bombarding him with text messages demanding his response, it won't go well for you. Reacting aggressively or like a possessive wife even before the start of a relationship can easily turn a guy off. Who would want the clingy and toxic type anyway?

Over analysis and overreaction are relationship killers— and between men and women, women tend to commit them more. In your case, it may mean nipping it in the bud. It simply means that you're already putting a potential relationship to an end even before it blossoms.

Remember that men aren't big fans of lengthy messages. For them, novel-like texts are dramas and they naturally stay away from those. They usually keep their responses short and replying in one to two words (e.g. awesome, okay, yep, hang on, sounds good, etc.) is quite normal for them. However, this doesn't actually mean that they're not interested in you.

Word of advice: Don't punish yourself overthinking about his short messages. Accept them at face value and if it really bothers you, have a good talk about it when you meet. You could drive yourself insane by thinking about everything he says. So relax and be casual. Don't worry about every single word or kiss in a message.

The magic of a random compliment.

We touched on this earlier, but just because you're now in a relationship doesn't mean you can stop paying him compliments. If anything, you should be doing this now more than ever as you try to keep that spark alive. Think of it this way, a compliment by text is a technological tool you can use to get closer to each other. Text him a compliment, even a small one, and it'll make him not only feel flattered, but he'll also feel more attracted to you because you know how to make him feel amazing.

Send those goodnight texts.

This can be an opportunity to get a little naughty, or it can remain sweet. Either way, texting him as you lie in bed just to say you're thinking about him will give him a warm fuzzy feeling as he knows he's on your mind as you drift off to sleep. And a goodnight text will make sure you're the last person he's thinking of.

Mad about something? Text it.

This is quite a controversial theory because I've read countless pieces of advice that insist arguments should take place face to face. This is because texting is seen as impersonal and even a little rude if you're trying to discuss something important. But, to some extent, I disagree.

Text messages can be an incredible tool when you're having an argument because you can say things you might not have the confidence to say if you're actually with a person. This means you can be more honest and not hide your feelings from each other.

But texts are also amazing at stopping your anger from destroying a relationship. This is because you actually have to take the time to type out a message and read it over before you send it. Meaning you're less likely to yell something out of anger that you don't mean and can't take back.

Texting brings a certain amount of calmness to an argument, so take advantage and tell him what you think. Just make sure to double check what you've written before you hit send. If in doubt, read the message out loud to hear what it would really sound like coming from you.

Set some boundaries.

This doesn't mean you have to organize a strict schedule, but it does mean being mindful and respectful of each other's commitments. If you can't text at work or during a class then make sure he knows that time of the day is off limits. Likewise if he has to be up for work early, don't pester him in the middle of the night.

Learn to know what works for you both and eventually, you'll have your own steady texting rhythm. Meanwhile, learn early on what you are both comfortable with when it comes to subject matter. Some couples are comfortable texting about everything from sex and horror movies to political issues and religion. But if any of these make you feel awkward, don't be afraid to tell him.

Always say thank you.

Taking the time to text your appreciation after a date will not only make you appear to be a kind and grateful person, but it will also make him happier than you can even imagine. Just knowing that you are thankful for the time you spent together will make him feel special and appreciated. And he'll be eager to repeat the experience!

Learn to take a break.

If you were with someone twenty-four hours a day, you might begin to get infuriated with each other and maybe even slightly bored. It's no different with texting. You don't have to be doing it every minute of the day. And it's true, absence *does* make the heart grow fonder.

Learn to take some time out from texting once in a while and don't feel as though you have to always be messaging each other. It's not healthy to be constantly chatting and it's definitely not practical, especially when you have to get something done. Take a break every now and again and let each other breathe. Even though you're now a couple, it doesn't mean you have to forget what it's like to lead individual lives.

Don't replace real conversations with texts.

Yes, texting is incredible and lets you keep in touch all the time. But it doesn't mean you have to let texting take over your relationship to the point that it replaces actually being together and speaking to one another. Texting should be something that helps build the relationship. It shouldn't actually *be* the relationship.

Learn when love turns to obsession.

There's one thing when you're texting regularly because you enjoy talking. Yet it's another thing entirely when either one of you is stifled by the amount of texts you're receiving. Texting to the point where it is starting to affect your life and your independence is not only completely unhealthy, it also isn't sustainable.

If your guy is texting you constantly to the point where you feel suffocated, it's time to start realizing he isn't just interested or in love with you. He's obsessed! And this type of obsession can be hugely harmful to a relationship as he becomes more and more dependent on you.

Meanwhile, if you find yourself dependent on your other half and can't got an hour, or even a minute, without texting him, then it's time to re-evaluate your feelings. Are you in love with him? Or are you jealous and possessive and need to know where he is all the time?

On one hand, if you find yourself obsessively texting, it could be a sign of an underlying emotional problem. Perhaps you are afraid of being abandoned or maybe you have anxiety that makes you feel as though you have to be in control and know his whereabouts all the time. If that is the case, you would benefit from talking to both your partner, and a professional. And it would be hugely beneficial to seek out techniques that can calm you down and stop you worrying about constantly reaching for your phone.

If you are anxious about hearing from your partner and are tempted to text him all the time, find ways to distract yourself. Play a game on your phone, busy yourself with a project or spend some time outside. Remember, you are your own person and your life shouldn't revolve around somebody else to the point where your relationship is growing unhealthy.

On the flip side, being an obsessive texter will only serve to push him away. If he's constantly getting dozens of messages from you throughout the day, he might be thinking, D*oes she not have anything better to do? Doesn't she work? Does she not have a life?*

This is far from a good look and will do little to make you appear attractive to him. Guys (and women) are attracted to people that are strong and independent and have their own lives, not someone who sits around all day waiting to hear back from you.

Ensure you both initiate conversations.

If it's always you that texts first then this might be a sign that things are starting to become a little unbalanced. Think about it. What would happen if you stopped being the first to initiate a conversation? Would he text you? Or would he simply disappear?

If you find that you're always the first person to chat then try a little experiment and stay quiet for a while. If he gets in touch then that's great and you know that maybe that was just how things were, and you developed a routine where you were always first. But if you don't hear a thing from him, then it's time to accept you were more interested in him than he was in you. It's difficult and it hurts, but it's better to know the truth.

Similarly, are you the kind of person that texts an entire essay to your man and only get back a measly '*cool*'. Loads of girls will say they've done this. And some of us guys too! But this can also be a sign that things are becoming lopsided in your relationship. You'll have to figure out if your long messages are maybe just intimidating him and putting him off speaking to you, or if he's just not a particularly wordy person.

Yet, it could be symptomatic of something more. Once again, it's time to decide if his level of interest matches yours. Play it cool and quiet for a while and quit with the long messages. If he responds accordingly, then you know he's still interested. But if his messages start to fizzle out even more, then it might be time to call it quits.

Text on an emotional level.

Memes are hilarious but you can't build a relationship on them. If you find that your texts are more banter than meaningful conversation then it might be time to consider if you are actually a loving couple, or whether you're just friends.

I'm not saying all your texts have to be romantic sonnets or that you have to have in-depth heart to hearts every day. But it is essential that your messages have some sort of emotional resonance to them so you know you care about each other. This can take the form of just asking how their day was, wondering how they are, asking about something they care about or saying how you feel about something. Maintaining this depth of communication will ensure you stay close and bond the more you talk.

Not only this, but you don't want to appear as though you're always talking about yourself without considering the other person. Text messages are supposed to be a two-way thing, not an opportunity for you to vent and empty out your thoughts until you bore the other person. Doing this will make them think you don't care about what they have to say and in turn, your lack of consideration for their feelings will only push you apart.

Couples can use texting as a form of emotional support for those days when you're not together. And just like in the example of arguments, it could actually be easier for you to voice your opinion in a text message if you're struggling to do it in person. But this can only be done if you're both interested in maintaining this emotional connection.

Don't second guess yourself.

Have you ever written a text then deleted it all? Have you even gone so far as to get your friends together in a group chat to craft the perfect text message to send a guy?

When you're nervous and trying to figure out the right thing to say to a guy, it can be too easy to fall into the trap of perfectionism. You'll fuss and freak out over every word, comma, capital letter and kiss. But the reality is, there is no perfect text message and chances are he won't see the flaws that you do. So all your fussing will have been for nothing.

Not only this, but the act of constantly second guessing yourself to the point of re-writing your texts and getting anxious over every tiny word, means there's something deeper at play here. This anxiety, although currently related to texting is more symptomatic of an underlying sense of low self-esteem. It's not the actual text message that's making you stress, it's what he'll think of you once you send it.

If you feel this to be the case, then it would be better to work on your self-confidence rather than your text messages. This is of course easier said than done, but there are many ways you can boost your confidence. My personal favourite way is to take deep breaths, close my eyes, relax and visualize myself as I want to be, rather than imagining myself with all my flaws. Do this regularly and you'll find you become more like the visualized version of yourself every day!

Be consistent.

When you fall into your texting routine and grow closer, you'll most likely find you will know when you will hear from each other. It won't be a formal agreement, but you'll get used to texting at a certain time of the day and then expect to hear from them. Every texting schedule and relationship is different. For some couples, they might text each other every evening, while for others it might be every few hours, or maybe even every week! There is no right or wrong way to have a consistent texting relationship. However, what is essential is that one exists.

There's nothing worse than waiting by the phone to hear from someone and not knowing if you'll be able to talk. It makes you nervous, it makes you feel neglected and in turn, it makes you feel pushed away and resentful. It doesn't matter how casual your texting routine is, but making sure you have one will add a sense of safety and trust to your relationship as you know when you will be able to rely on each other. Whether that be for a quick word, a silly joke or something more serious.

As we've seen, navigating the complexities of texting within a relationship can be an emotional minefield and sometimes, it can feel like hard work. But there are two things that can help guide you through the tricky process. First, if you find yourself stressing and panicking about texting, whether that be what you say or when you've heard from him, then there is something unhealthy and unbalanced within your relationship. Texting should be a tool to help you get closer, not something that should stress you out.

Meanwhile, let your gut instinct guide you. It may sound simple, but there's nothing more powerful than your own internal ability to gauge how the relationship is going. If you feel something is not quite right and there are peculiarities presenting themselves in your text messages, then take note.

WHAT TEXTS DO GUYS WANT TO SEE?

Okay, we've covered the basics of what *you* should do, and how you should talk and text him, but what does *he* actually want? And what exactly do men think about texting? Are they just like women and over think everything?

Well, in some ways, yes, guys worry about the same things. A recent online thread dedicated to how men text revealed they panic just as much as women do. We are also prone to the same emotional ups and downs that women suffer from when they're trying to get someone's attention. However, one thing that this thread revealed was that pretty much all guys admit their texting habits change significantly when they're texting a woman that they like, rather than when they're just speaking to their buddies or family.

Let's take a look at some of these changes now and see if you can spot them in your guy. You never know, you might even recognize some of these traits in yourself.

How do guys change their texting habits if they like you?

1. They become more attentive

It's easy to imagine guys as being a little cold and aloof, especially if they love playing the part of a bad boy. But generally, guys get just as excited about texting back as women do and often have to hold back to not seem desperate. Sound familiar?

One thing men report is that when they like a woman, they automatically *want* to text, whereas before they most likely replied to their friends with a single word or a funny meme. Now, however, they find their behaviour changing because they're trying to impress a woman, not an old pal. Self-confessed 'bad texters' now become the best conversationalists in the world. As one poster on a well-known men's forum said - *"After reading a text from a woman I'm like: "just play it cool, man.... You don't have to respond right away... Oh f**k it; just send it."*

It may comfort you to know us guys feel just as nervous as you. After all, we have the same thoughts, concerns and worries about dating. This means you can learn to relax knowing that whatever you're thinking, he's thinking it too. What is also fun is that you can tell right away if a guy likes you because if he's taking the time to actually talk to you, and to not text you like he would a friend, you must be special to him.

2. He starts to enjoy the constant conversation

It's usually assumed women are the chattiest, but if a guy likes you, this just isn't the case. Most guys report that once they like a woman, and they begin texting, they love the constant flow of texts and conversation. It makes us super excited and we find that the need for conversation is totally different with a woman we are attracted to in comparison with just a friend. For example, guys will say that if they lose interest in a conversation, they'll usually just stop responding, but with a woman they like, they're more eager to keep the conversation flowing.

So what does this tell us? Well, first, it lets us know we shouldn't be afraid to engage in conversation. Secondly, it tells you that a guy's need to engage in meaningful discussion is just as prominent as yours.

3. He begins using a filter

Not the kind of filter to make our photos more flattering, but the type that makes him think more about what he says and how it will affect you. Many guys will tell you that when they're talking to friends, they'll chat about anything and everything without worrying about the consequences. But this all goes out the window the moment they start texting an attractive woman. Now they're thinking about everything they say and are keen to make sure we're not offending you or coming across as stupid. They see this as a way to, not just make sure they're not putting you off, but as a way to put in the extra effort they think you deserve.

4. *He gets nervous*

Yes, we get nervous too when waiting for a response! This shouldn't be so surprising, but for some, it really is a shock to think that the cute guy who always comes across as super-confident and even sometimes a little cocky, could be nervous about hearing from you. One guy in a recent online survey said that he got so nervous texting a woman that after he replied to her, he would toss his phone across the room until he built up the courage to read her reply.

Guys are just like women when it comes to their texting habits. We over think things just like you do. We get anxious, start moderating the way we speak and love to engage in conversation as much as you do. Hopefully, what the above can teach you is that you can relax a little and not place the guy you're texting on a pedestal. A guy's concerns are just like yours and they have the same worries. Believe me, no matter how nervous you are about how you come across and what he's thinking of you, his stomach will be doing somersaults just like yours.

Learn to use this to your advantage. Think of him as someone who is thinking and feeling the way you are, and you'll eventually start to realize there's nothing to be nervous about at all.

Okay, so now we know how he's feeling, but what exactly does he want? Sometimes, people focus so much on all the science and social complications of a conversation that we forget on what people actually want to see.

Here, we cover 5 types of texts that men actually want to receive. So get your pens ready and take note!

5 Texts men actually want to receive

Upfront texts

No messing around, no hidden meanings, no mind games. Just straight up, blunt and open messages that let him know exactly what you're thinking. It looks a little something like this:

You. Me. Drinks downtown tonight.

Or even better.

My place. Eight o'clock. Be there.

You can even get a little bolder and dirtier depending on how comfortable you are, and how long you've known each other. I doubt there are many guys out there who could resist a message like this:

Just out the shower. Wanna give me a back rub? ;)

It sends your intentions loud and clear and men love the no-nonsense attitude and the confidence it exudes. Men also love this kind of message because it defies the rules. He'll be expecting the anxiety-riddled back and forth that slowly builds up to an invitation, but an upfront text smashes that to pieces and gets right to the point.

Receiving a text like that will make you appear confident, in control and not like anyone else. Even if that's the opposite of what you're feeling.

However, what you have to watch is that your confident message doesn't come across as arrogant, and there's a fine line between sassiness and stubbornness. He'll love your confidence, but he'll also appreciate it if you appear to want to meet his needs.

A little bonus tip is that if you are brave enough to send a message like this, make sure to keep a little mystery. You can be seductive and tease him, but don't let him know right away if he'll get lucky or not. Make him work a little and make him wait.

Spontaneous fun facts

This may seem a little random, and maybe even a bit silly, but bear with me. Revealing a quirky side to you not only keeps him on his toes as he learns new and interesting things about you, but it can also provide him with an excuse to hang out with you. Take this for an example:

Hey, fun fact. I'm super into collecting vinyl and I know you love music too. Wanna meet up and go record digging with me?

Or

I love scary movies. Wanna come check that new one out with me?

Men love this kind of message because it's an instant ice-breaker, and lets him know something interesting and personal about you. Relationship expert, Iona Yeung says this kind of message serves two purposes. First, it takes the pressure off the guy to think of something to say or having to initiate a conversation. While it also gives him a dose of cheekiness that leaves the door open for some serious flirting. Think of it this way, a message like that could get as fun and raunchy as you want.

Hey, fun fact. I love it when...

You can go anywhere with a message like this if you're bold enough. What a text like this also does is to emphasise what you like and therefore what you're good at and where your strengths lie. Whether that be showing an artistic flair or being dynamite on a running track. Sending him a text with a fun fact puts you right in the driving seat and makes you appear confident and highly attractive as you talk about what really makes you... you. A little fact about yourself might seem small and trivial to you, but to him, it will show just how much you rock.

However, one thing you should never do is to make up a fact and lie about yourself. The last thing you should do is tell him you're super into race car driving when you haven't even passed your test, or that you're an excellent mountain climber when you're actually terrified of heights. Just be yourself!

The invitation that's not actually an invitation

First, this kind of text is amazing for women because it makes you take the lead without appearing domineering or desperate. You can take control without looking as though you're trying too hard. An example of one of these messages looks like this:

I'm at a great party right now. I thought you were gonna be here. Are you coming?

Or,

I'm watching this amazing movie on TV right now. Would have been cool if you were here to share this enormous pizza I just ordered.

One thing he'll love about this kind of text is that it makes you appear as though you've got your own thing going on, but you wish he would be a part of your plans. It'll make him feel special that you're thinking about him when you're having so much fun. But not only that, it'll send a pretty clear signal of where you want him to be, but without the pressure and anxiety of actually asking him out.

Yeung says these kinds of texts work like magic because if a guy loves to feel chased, then he has your attention. But if he loves to be doing the chasing, then you've given him a gentle tease and a prompt to come get you. Not only that, but it'll make him feel as though turning up to meet you was *his* idea. Genius!

Just make sure that you don't play games. If you actually wanted to hang out with him at that party, then you have to make sure you're really there and not just messing around. Follow through on the invitation in your text, even if it wasn't a real and proper invitation to start with.

Secondly, don't keep texting him all night with more and more teasing invitations while dropping constant hints. If he doesn't take the bait, or worse, doesn't reply, just let it go.

Messages straight from the heart

These have the same impact as the upfront, no-nonsense text messages that men love because they're brutally honest. I'm not saying you have to divulge a personal secret, or say something you don't want to, but sending a meaningful message straight from your heart will go right to his. Think of how powerful a message like this is:

Couldn't stop thinking about you today.

Or,

Had a great night with you. Wish you didn't have to leave.

There's something both sweet and strong about a message like this because it hides nothing and gets straight to the point, but simultaneously shows a vulnerable side to you.

Believe me, this is a good thing, and vulnerability doesn't have to mean that you look like a lesser person or that he will view you as weak. If anything, displaying your vulnerability is a strength and shows that you are not afraid to have real, human feelings. Sometimes, men don't feel as though they can engage with this sensitive side of life, so he'll appreciate you reaching out with a message that portrays both affection and emotion.

Sending a text like this will make him feel special and he'll be saving it on his phone to revisit time and time again. Yet it also solidifies the roles you play in each other's life. If you're communicating to him that you can't stop thinking about him, and that he's now a big part of your life, he'll also be thinking that you're a big part of his.

However, you do have to make sure that you actually mean what you say. Don't tell him that he's always on your mind if he's not. That will just lull him into a false sense of security and lead him on. Instead, text him something you really mean and in turn, you will receive meaningful engagement from him.

Meanwhile, save a text like this for when you've known him for a little while. Not only will it have more impact, but it will seem less peculiar than if you were to send it right after your first date.

Ask for his opinion

Generally, people feel important whenever they're asked for their opinion so they're usually willing to give it. Showing him that his opinion matters to you helps you establish a bond with him. Texting becomes more fun and worthwhile.

Give more focus to "listening" to his perspectives than your own. Use open-ended questions. This way, you can make him expand his answers instead of getting replies limited to "yeah," "I guess so," "you could say that," or "no." Look at these examples:

- What do you think about the latest episode of TWD?
- What do you say about Brazil's performance in the last game?
- So you've seen Conjuring 3, how was it?
- Why do you think they let him win?

- Why didn't you like their performance?

Give him your ATM updates

In the internet lingo, ATM stands for "At The Moment." You can send him photos and texts telling him what you're up to. This can make your conversation more interesting and can give him cues about yourself (e.g. hobbies, abilities, interests, etc.). It can also bring you two closer with each other by letting him be more engaged in your life. Let's give you a few ideas:

- Him: Busy?
- You: Just a bit. I'm trying to bake your favorite blueberry cheesecake.
- Him: Shame that I can't even have a bite :(
- You: Come over. I'll save you a slice or two ;)
- "I'm having lunch in my favorite resto. How about u?"
- Photo of you working out with the caption, "Trying to stay fit. #BeMyWorkoutBuddy"

Just a little reminder— exercise moderation. Don't overwhelm him with blow-by-blow updates. It also helps to focus more on knowing what he's doing than concentrating the conversation in what's going on with you. Make him realize that he's a participant in your tête-à-tête instead of a mere reader.

Be the supportive textmate

Confidence and success are usually attained through a healthy mindset, and a healthy mindset can be achieved through an individual's personal efforts and other outside factors like support from his loved ones. Be a driving force that can push him to be a better version of himself. If he has a job interview, an upcoming big project or an important life event, let him know that you're there to support him. Even a small pep talk via text message every day makes a huge difference in how he could welcome his daily challenges. Here are some samples how you can wish him the best of luck:

- "Good luck on your job interview today. Go get ,'em!"
- "Relax. Victory is already ours. The meeting's just a formality."
- "Today's not 'yet another day.' It's our day to shine." (Insert a good encouraging meme or your photo with a big, bright smile.)

Ask for an update

Paying attention to details about his adventures, hobbies or activities can give you ideas for your next topic. It will likewise show him that you do care even about the little details of his life. Ask what happened to his recent trip or project. Below are samples of what you can ask:

- "Hey, how was your homecoming on Thanksgiving?"
- "So, about the client u told me about last time. Were you able to close the deal?"
- "Tell me about your adventures in Japan. I'm dying to know!"
- "Is your mom okay now? I hope she gets well soon."
- "How was your 'kitchen experiment'? Everything fine?"

The Ultimate Flirt

Both guys and girls love to flirt, and Yeung thinks that the best way to send a flirty message is to mix a recipe of 2 magic elements; a lashing of sexual innuendo and a liberal sprinkling of humour. The key is to keep things sexy, fun and light-hearted. So what does one of these magic flirty texts look like? Well, there are multiple ways you can send one and they don't always have to be raunchy. In fact, figuring out which flirty text to send can be a little bit of an art. In fact, some relationships experts believe there are multiple categories of flirty texts. Let's take a look at them now.

The Flirty Question

These are the ones that put you in control as you can set the mood and tone of the conversation. Examples are:

Wanna know a dirty secret?

What would you say if I kissed you?

I miss you and wish you were here. What are you going to do about it?

Referencing Previous Dates.

These not only strengthen the relationship because you're reminding him of a time when you had fun together, but they also encourage the need for more dates. Examples these messages look like this:

Can't stop thinking about the way you looked in that shirt last night.

Last weekend was so much fun. Can't stop thinking about it.

Referencing Future Dates.

Keep him expecting more, and make sure to add that dash of innuendo.

I picked my outfit for tomorrow. Want a sneak peak?

Can't wait until our next date. I've been looking forward to it all week ;)

Get X-rated

If you're comfortable with this and you trust your guy, don't be afraid to dial things right up. A sexy text will really amp things up and set his pulse racing.

Can't stop thinking about all the things I could do to you.

If you send me a sexy selfie, I might have to send one back.

Wanna know a secret? I'm not wearing any underwear.

These kinds of flirty messages will rev his engine and will soon set sparks flying. The key is to keep them short and sweet and always fun. Don't over think things, don't analyse every word. Just say what you're thinking and you'll be sure to get what you want.

Add a little bit of mystery

Guys love mystery, the sense of the unknown waiting to be deciphered but you don't have to force it in every single way. While you might have shared your secret or be the carefree beauty who stole everybody's attention, that doesn't mean that you have to be an open book that everybody can read.

When asking something personal, instead of giving him a direct answer, drop him a puzzle that returns the question back at him. Or limit your stories about yourself to ignite his interest in you more. Remember that less is more which is what you should be actually doing.

You don't need to make him feel that you're at his beck and call. As much as possible; stay normal. You may indulge in long texting session with him at times when you have enough time and in an appropriate place. You don't need to get away from whatever it is you're doing just because he texted. In this case, results can be drastic and the odds will be in your favor.

If everything went well, it's just a matter of time before he will be asking you out on a date. This brings us to the next phase of our action plan. So, let's first address what's arguably the most important question for our succeeding move: "Who does the texting first?"

There's no concrete rule as to who does the texting first. As previously stated in the last chapter, men are attracted to assertive women but here's the catch: don't be too pushy.

Make him want to meet you again soon

Condition his mind with text messages suggesting another meet-up. Be subtle and make sure you don't sound too eager about it. Open-ended suggestions work best as this trick stimulates his desire to see you as well. Take a look at these samples:

- I really had a good time talking with you last time. One of the best nights in like forever :)
- I love action movies. Speaking of which, there's an upcoming Jason Statham movie next weekend.
- Well, I love cooking pasta. I think I'll make chicken Alfredo or carbonara for dinner tomorrow so…
- There's a new Italian restaurant I want to visit. Want to hang out there some time?
- What are you doing this weekend? I have the complete DVD sets of Resident Evil and The Fast & the Furious.

Let his imagination run wild

Do you know what's charming about text-flirting? You can tease his imagination and make him wild with longing for you—that is if you play it right. There's no perfect formula for this, but that's the thrill. What you just need to learn is to send him harmless, seemingly innocent text messages but can be interpreted in a lot of ways.

Here's the trick: Text him something that could tickle his dirty mind. Below are some examples:

- Gotta go get some shower ;) TTYL

- Oh, my... I've spilled some water on my white top.
- Just got home. I went lingerie shopping with my BFFs.
- I think I need aromatherapy for my bath tonight. What do u think?
- Haven't done my laundry. Looks like I don't have anything to wear...
- My 30-day diet paid off. I think I like what I see in the mirror now...
- What do you think should I wear for the party? Little black dress or backless beige gown?
- Guess what? I just bought a bikini for Ann's beach party.

Know How to Manage his Naughty Text Messages

There are times when a guy would send you naughty or dirty text messages when you're able to tickle his wild side. As a mature woman, you must know how to respond without stepping out of your boundaries. Remember, there's a fine line between texting dirty and flirty texting. Cross this line and you'll reap unfavorable consequences.

So what do you do when he begins to send you naughty or dirty text messages? Study the conversations below.

- **You:** Just got home. I went lingerie shopping with my BFFs.

- **Him:** So, when can I see you in it? Better yet, without it?
- **You:** I can see a naughty little boy. Christmas is approaching and Santa's making a list of those who are naughty and nice ;)
- **You:** I think I need aromatherapy for my bath tonight. What do u think?
- **Him:** Here's what I think— me in the tub with you.☐
- **You:** Silly boy ;) Give me a minute, I think my pasta is already done. (And don't text him until he texts you again. Better yet, text him the next day when he's already calmed down.)

Instead of completely shutting him off, you put him back to his place in a playful way without hurting his feelings or sounding too condescending in the process.

WHAT DO GUYS **NOT** WANT?

Okay, so now we know what we should say to get his motor running, but is there anything you shouldn't text him? The answer is yes. There are multiple things women do via text that not only annoy him, but are likely to push him away. But don't worry because we're going to cover them now so you can make sure you're pulling him closer to you, not forcing him further away.

The Top 4 Turn Offs

In 2015, a survey was conducted by Match.com to reveal a plethora of information about people's texting habits and how attractive (or unattractive) they make you appear. For guys, the 3 biggest turn offs were:

- **Typos and bad grammar.** with 33% of male participants stating a terrible use of language being the ultimate turn off.

- **Short answers like 'K'.** I'll admit, receiving this one letter reply is just about the most infuriating message you could ever receive as a guy! In fact, 33% of participants reported it was their biggest turn off.

- **CONSTANTLY WRITING IN ALL CAPS.** I don't know why someone would write all their messages like this, but apparently there are plenty of people who do because 30% of men surveyed said it made them run for the hills.

- **Being texted at work.** We discussed this earlier with setting boundaries and making sure there is a healthy space between you. For guys, there will always be a time when texting is off limits. For some of us, it's late at night while for others it's during family time. For 47% of men, it's during their working day, and they reported that they simply hated being texted at work.

(Interestingly, as a side note, 70% of both sexes surveyed stated that a huge turn off was their date having their phone on the table during a dinner date.)

Boring conversation

It's bad enough having to make small talk at the best of times. I mean, who wants to talk about the weather or what they're having for dinner. But boring chat is even worse in a text message and makes a guy think you're as dull as dishwater.

Sending boring texts might not be the worst sin you can commit in the dating world, however, it sends up a red flag to a guy. This is because when you're flirting with a guy over a text, you're supposed to be presenting your A-game and making a good impression, you're not supposed to be boring the pants off him. If he's getting texts from you talking about picking out shades of wallpaper then he'll be thinking this is the best conversation you have to offer.

I'm not saying you have to be sending him the most incredible, fascinating messages of all the time, but you at least have to be passionate and interested in what you're talking about.

Texting Too Often

This is pretty obvious, but worth reiterating because one of the biggest turn offs for guys is getting absolutely bombarded with text after text. Especially when they're about nothing in particular.

It can be easy to get carried away and text too much. Some of us guys have been there too, but make sure to pay attention. If the number of messages between you becomes unbalanced, it's worth reining yourself in so you don't put him off. If you're in doubt, back off for a little while and if he's interested, he'll get back in touch.

Not Texting Enough.

Okay, so this is when it gets confusing. I thought you said I was texting too much, I hear you complain. Well, the opposite can also be true and sometimes, if you're trying to play hard to get, you can appear rude and disinterested. If a guy sees that you're barely replying, he'll be thinking it's because they've done something wrong. This means his ego will be taking a battering, and it's up to you to make him feel good again.

I know it's frustrating, and there's a fine line between texting too much and too little, but the key, in my humble opinion, is to match them text for text rather than firing off 3 in quick succession or ignoring them completely. It's all about balance, reciprocation, and paying attention to the flow of the conversation.

Vague Messages

Has a guy ever texted you a question and you've replied with a series of ambiguous emoji instead of words? Has he ever asked you out on a date and you've replied with something cryptic and confusing? These are the texting equivalent of a shrug and they drive him crazy, and not in a good way.

Guys are hard-wired to see things clearly and they need clear answers, not brain teasers. Be as simple as possible and shy away from non-sensical and immature emoji. If he pays you a compliment, don't respond with a series of hearts, a cactus, a pair of shoes and a random vegetable. Just say what you mean!

Dismissing Their Compliments

It requires a certain amount of emotional energy for a guy to pluck up the courage to send you a compliment. As you know, men aren't always the easiest of creatures to open up, so when they do, you know they really mean it. That's why they get so infuriated when they compliment you and you simply ignore them.

A guy texting you a compliment, or being sensitive in general, is a way in which they are showing you their vulnerable side, and that's a big deal. It shows he trusts you and is willing to drop the macho facade. When you ignore these compliments, they don't see why they should bother to give you another one, and they'll think you're being rude.

I'm not saying you have to present him with a medal every time he tells you you're pretty, but a simple thank you will show that his compliment was at least noted.

Complaints about the 'Seen' Receipt

I totally get it. When you see someone has read your message but hasn't replied, it makes you disheartened, disappointed, and makes you feel ignored. Your mind starts racing as you panic that you've said something wrong, that you've offended him, or maybe he's got bored of you and has moved on. But it's important to remember there could be a whole host of reasons why he hasn't replied.

Not to mention, complaining to him about keeping you on 'read' will only make you look clingy and, to be honest, a little creepy. He'll think you spend all day staring at the screen waiting for him. Which is never a good look. If he doesn't reply, try not to worry about it. As hard as that might be, it'll be worth it in the long-run. Chasing him up for not replying to you fast enough will only make him run away.

Compliment Fishing

Texting to tell him how fat and ugly you feel will not have the effect you want it to. I understand in an image conscience world you might feel as though you need his approval. But deliberately putting yourself down so he can build you back up will make you look insecure at best, and manipulative at worst. Usually, texts like this will only make him lose interest in you, and fast.

Negging

Have you ever heard of the negging phenomenon? If you haven't, I'd count yourself lucky. Negging is when a pick-up artist will deliberately insult you to get you into bed. It seems like it would have the opposite effect for most people, but that actually isn't the case. What normally occurs is that this psychological trick will lower your self-esteem so much that you will end up chasing after the person dishing out the insults because you'll become desperate for their approval.

Used mostly by guys and nearly always by narcissists, it has become a well-known trick among pick-up forums. It's just about the cruellest form of flirting there is and doesn't just occur among male pick-up artists.

Women are also known to take part in negging. Although they might not do it with the specific goal of getting a guy into bed, they'll more than likely do it to make a man feel small and useless. This is so they can lead them on and have them hanging on their every word in order to seek their approval.

Negging might not be something you do on purpose. It might not even be something you've even heard of, but perhaps you find yourself reaching to that part of your brain that's willing to dish out an insult in order to gain control. Or maybe you're just sending insults because you're frustrated and can't communicate your thoughts in a clearer, more civilized way.

Insults are not attractive and they are only going to make him want to distance himself from you. If you find yourself becoming snappy, even if you don't mean to, take a deep breath, learn to control your anger, and think of something pleasant to say. And if you can't do that, just don't say anything at all.

RESOLVING CONFLICT THROUGH TEXT

As much as we'd like to think all relationships are easy, they sadly aren't. People have differences of opinion and experience emotions differently. This all means that arguments are an inevitability within a relationship. And that's completely normal! Even the closest, most loving couples argue from time to time. As long as it's not a daily occurrence, there's really nothing to worry about. Arguments, or at least disagreements can be healthy. After all, if we just went around agreeing with what our partner said all the time, it would be a little odd at best, and would breed resentment at worst. What I'm saying is, you'd be quite an anomaly if you didn't have at least one argument throughout your relationship.

People of an older generation, who didn't grow up with cell phones would most likely tell you that conflict should be resolved face to face. They might even tell you that texting has no place in a relationship and that all interaction should take place in person.

However, if you've read this far I'm guessing you don't share this way of thinking. These days, texting permeates all our relationships and it has become a normal part of everyday life as much as breathing (well, for most of us anyway). Therefore, it's expected that texting will not only play a central role in your romantic relationships, but will also play a huge part in how you resolve problems in these relationships.

Whether you believe that conflict should be resolved in person or not, or that we're relying too much on technology, the fact of the matter is that in this modern world, we'll have to have an argument through text at some point.

But it doesn't have to be impersonal, and it definitely doesn't have to be rude and insensitive. Having an argument through text can have its benefits. In fact, for some people, it can even be easier than doing it face to face. As I mentioned previously, there are 2 factors that make it easier than arguing in person. First, you can say things you might not be brave enough to say if that person was standing right in front of you. And second, you can take your time to type out a message and think carefully about what you're saying instead of blurting out something hurtful that you'll later regret.

So let's have a look at how we can resolve conflict through texts. It's easier than you think and there's a pretty simple formula you can follow to make sure your disagreements don't only come to an end, but that the both of you work toward a solution for your problems.

First, remember that although you might be arguing through the use of modern technology, you can still use traditional methods of communication your grandma would certainly approve of. For instance, all the technology in the world could never replace the need for the following helpful and respectful social skills.

The Basics

- **Don't hurl insults.** They shouldn't be a way for you to unleash your anger on your other half. This will only lead to hurt feelings, regret, and emotional wounds that may take a long time to heal. Instead, when you know you are having a disagreement, make the aim of the conversation be the quest for a solution to your problems.

This means that you are not against your partner and the notion of you vs. them has been eliminated. Instead, think of it as you and your partner vs. the problem. This will mean you are together in a search for the answer, rather than against each other trying to score points.

- **Have a cool off period.** This is actually easier to do if you are texting because you can simply tell them you need some space and place your phone somewhere that isn't right under your nose. Making sure you both have time to cool off will ensure that neither of you let your emotions run the show, and that you are both re-entering the conversation with a fresh, cool mind. Never let your anger dictate what you say. It will only lead you to say things in the heat of the moment, and nothing you say in this state has a good outcome.

- **Be honest**. This goes without saying. If you were together in person, you would be expected to display honesty. And it's no different in text messages. Honesty will not only bring a faster resolution to the disagreement, but it will also build trust between you and your partner and bring you closer together.

Sometimes it's difficult to be honest because you are ashamed of what you want to say or you worry that you'll make your other half angry. But the truth is that you are most likely building up and magnifying your thoughts so that something you've been holding back has reached catastrophic proportions in your head. In reality, they won't be as big a deal as you think they are, and could even be quickly resolved if you voice your troubles to your partner.

- **Be respectful.** This is another obvious one but worth emphasizing. Just because your man isn't right in front of you, it doesn't mean you should say things to him that you wouldn't normally. But respect also goes further than just watching what you say. Being respectful to your partner means you listen carefully to what they say and give them time to speak. It means you acknowledge their complaints, even if you don't agree, and it means approaching a disagreement with a sense of understanding. In essence, respect means having patience and putting your own feelings temporarily to the side to really listen and pay attention to what someone's saying.

With the basics covered, you can now start to look at the formula you can implement to ensure your argument comes to a swift and simple resolution. It's as easy as following the letters R – I – S – C. Let's go over what these mean here.

The RISC Technique

- **R = Report.** This doesn't mean drawing up a formal document. It does, however, mean you report on what has happened. This should be straight forward in a text message as you can begin outlining what is bothering you in a simple list. Whether you think your partner has done something to upset you, or maybe something happened between the two of you and you want to explain why it upset you, reporting the straight up facts will go a long way to not only explain how you feel, but to present your argument in a clear, concise way.

Remember what I said about men needing clear answers? Well, this is the perfect time to remember that. Guys aren't going to want ambiguous, cryptic text messages that don't fully explain why you are angry. They want your issue sketched out in a diagram if necessary and preferably with flashing lights.

But reporting the facts doesn't have to just be your responsibility. If he has a problem, tell him to outline his concerns in an understandable, transparent manner. This first step in resolving an argument is vital and will make sure you stay on track, rather than getting angry and going off on a tangent.

Ever had an emotionally charged argument and ended up ranting about a thousand other things? One moment you're arguing about why you're running late and the next thing you know you're screaming about who did the dishes two Sundays ago. We've all done it because it's too easy to try and score points and reply to your partner's comments about yourself with one about them. But this method of reporting the actual facts of what is taking place will get rid of that entirely.

- **I = Impact.** This means stating the actual impact of his actions. For example, when you did ___ it made me feel ___. What is so important about this is that, in contrast to just reporting the facts of the event, it actually shows its emotional consequences. What this does is make him see the precise impact of his actions. It could be that he was just being careless and genuinely didn't realize he was hurting you. If that's the case, then it's as straight forward as him acknowledging this impact and vowing to be more thoughtful in the future.

Meanwhile, he can also outline the impact of an event on his emotions. Not only will this make you realize how he is feeling, it will also give you a deeper insight into his thoughts and personality. But together, if you both perform this exercise, you will find that although it is difficult at first, it will bond you and make you closer than ever.

- **S = Specifics.** This doesn't just mean be specific about things in general, although that is definitely something to aim for. Remember when we covered how guys hate vague answers? But in this instance, being specific requires you to specify in exact terms how you want things to be. For example, do you want to change something about your partner? Do you want to change something about yourself? If that's the case, tell him in a clear way and you'll be able to move forward without any misunderstandings.

- **C = Consequences.** It's a scary word in any scenario but especially is in a relationship. Consequences mean something has happened that has changed your relationship and it means coming to terms with those changes. Yet, it doesn't have to be so scary. There can also be positive consequences, or negative ones that will change things for the better in the long run. The most important thing is to acknowledge them and understand how they occurred. For example, if this happens, the consequences will look like ___. Or if we can't resolve our problems then ___ will happen.

The above RISC strategy might appear intimidating, or might even look like too much hard work. But it doesn't have to be. These four steps will ensure any disagreements you have can be brought to a speedy resolution with as little impact as possible on your emotions.

However, I would like to provide a word of caution. Arguing through text can be incredibly helpful, and the technological aspect of having to only look at your screen can act as an emotionally protective barrier between you and your partner. For some people, this works out great, but for others, it might not. Don't feel that resolving disagreements through text is the only way to do it. If you feel that you'd rather voice your concerns in person and that way works for you then stick to it. If, however, you are used to resolving disputes through text, and it's a method that works great for you and your partner, then the RISC strategy can definitely help you.

WHAT DO YOU DO WHEN IT DOESN'T WORK OUT?

As much as we'd like relationships to run smoothly, sometimes they just don't, and sometimes, one person in the relationship is hell-bent on causing trouble or playing mind games. There's nothing more frustrating, or upsetting, than being genuine and sincere with someone only for them to blow hot and cold on you and lead you on one second before letting you down the next.

Maybe the guy you've spent so long trying to get the attention of isn't as sincere and caring as you hoped he was. But how do you know if you're being played? Are you worried he has lost interest? Or worse, are you starting to think you should let him go?

Don't worry because we've got you covered. In this chapter, we'll be covering 3 issues; how to know if he's playing games with you, what to do if he's lost interest, and we'll also be broaching the dreaded subject of breaking up through text.

How to know if he's playing games

Not all guys play games. In fact, many don't and are just interested in impressing you the good old fashioned way with some gentlemanly charm. But what happens when you fall for that one guy who's a total player, the kind that loves to mess women around and make them second guess themselves? Here, we take a look at 11 ways you can figure out if he's playing games.

1. **He always tries to keep the upper hand.** You know the type. They're always trying to stay in control and be in charge of everything. This often means they want to be the dominant one in the relationship who's intent on being the center of attention. They can try to do this by putting you down; belittling you and making you feel smaller and therefore inferior to them. He might even try to make you jealous of other women so you're worried you could lose him to someone else.

   Guys like this thrive off your constant attention and can become manipulative. They'll do anything to make you think they're God's gift to women and that you're lucky to have them. They'll be texting you one minute then ignoring you the next, and they might even have the audacity to text other women right in front of you.

   If you've got a guy like this you can do two things. You can either get rid of him and find someone who will respect and value you and appreciate your attention. Or you can play him right back! Don't fall for his games and resist his desire for you to show jealousy. Turn the tables on him and make him struggle to get your attention.

   2. **He flirts with other women.** There's a difference between being chatty with other women and having close female friends. Yet it's another thing entirely to flirt with other women, especially in front of you. This is a

deliberate ploy to make you jealous and insecure and sadly, for a lot of women, it will work and they'll strive to please him even more. But don't fall for it. If he's acting single when he says he's with you, then he clearly doesn't respect your relationship. Tell him it's either just you, or it's not you at all.

3. **He's always lying.** This has got to be one of the biggest red flags. A guy who lies is a guy you simply can't trust. If you find that he's texting you to say he's in one place when he's in another, or he texts you things about himself that turn out later to be untrue, then you know it's time to call it quits. A guy who lies like this will not give you a happy, long-term relationship. In fact, it's more likely that things are just going to get worse between you. You won't be able to trust him, he'll be more likely to cheat and emotionally abuse you and generally just make your life unbearably unhappy. If you find that he's constantly lying to you, do not tolerate it.

4. **He's hot and cold.** This could be that he's super-attentive one minute then absent the next or that he's happy with you one day then suddenly turns moody and unresponsive. Either way, unbalanced behaviour that makes you not know where you stand with him signals he's up to something.

Players love to go hot and cold to keep you on your toes. They'll thrive off your insecurities and enjoy every second of you chasing him. You'll be always trying to figure out what you've done wrong and wondering why he's not texting you back when he was so keen on you earlier. Don't stand for it. Tell him to make up his mind if he's interested or not.

5. **He makes you have dates in the same place.** Does he always suggest you go to the same nightclub or the same restaurant? There could be a reason for this. It could be because he wants to see you in a place he's comfortable, however, it's also a tactic of seasoned players. Guys who play games will have a specific scene rehearsed that they use time and time again. He'll know exactly what, when and where to do all the things he's practiced and knows what will work on a woman. He might even be taking you to the same places because he's found somewhere he doesn't know anyone and he's keeping you a secret from them.

If you want to know what he's really like, force him out of his comfort zone and take him somewhere you want to go. If he says no, then take it as a warning that he's hiding something from you. Or worse, hiding you from someone else.

6. **He makes you desperate for his approval.** We covered this earlier with the subject of

negging. Breaking someone down so they will do anything to please you and gain your approval is the sure fire tactic of a player. In essence, he'll always play hard to get so you have to work for his attention. He'll be texting you and keeping up a steady flow of conversation before keeping you on 'read' for hours so you spend the night staring at your phone wondering what you've done wrong and how you can win his attention back. What he doesn't realize is that he's lucky to have your attention and if anything, he should be chasing your approval. Don't let him make you feel unworthy of his attention.

7. **He gives you back-handed compliments.** These are a peculiar mix of an insult and a compliment such as:

You must be really brave to wear a dress that tight with those wide hips.

Or,

I love how you don't care about what your hair looks like.

Ouch. These are specifically designed to initially sound as though he's being a good guy and paying you a compliment when he's really chipping away at your self-confidence with a thinly veiled insult. This is a classic negging technique used by pick-up artists and is used for the sole purpose of making you feel terrible about yourself so you cherish his attention even more. Don't fall for them and let him know right away that you can see right through his games.

8. **He hates when you say no.** Does he quickly turn nasty if he doesn't get his own way? Does he act as though you should bend to his will at every chance and be grateful for the opportunity to fall at his feet? Chances are you're dating an egocentric narcissist who's simply not used to someone saying no and spits his dummy out when a woman uses the forbidden word. Guys like this will twist every situation where you say no so you look like the bad guy. He'll try to guilt trip you into saying yes to all his demands and generally doesn't respect your wishes or your choice to say no. But not only does he not respect your right to say no to him, he most likely doesn't respect you or women in general.

9. **He makes you wait.** He makes you think he's going to text you then leaves you hanging. Or worse, he says he'll meet you then stands you up! No guy would treat you this way if he wasn't playing games and you deserve better. Keeping you waiting or ignoring you completely is a move he's playing to make sure he's in control and you're always chasing him. Don't let him get away with it. If he enjoys ignoring your texts to make you lust

after him, make him know there are plenty of other guys who'll treat you better. And the first time he doesn't show up, make sure it's the last.

10. He doesn't call you his girlfriend. So you've been texting for a few months and have even gone out for a few dates. Things are getting steamy and you're definitely more than friends, but for some reason, every time you mention the word 'girlfriend' he clams up. So what's going on?

You're probably concocting all sorts of scenarios in your head. Does he not actually like me? Does he already have a girlfriend? It's not difficult to imagine that he's playing games with you. So what can you do? First, you have to figure out if he's terrified of the idea of a relationship because he has either been hurt in the past or whether he's scared of the idea of commitment. If that's the case, there are two things you can do. You can either help him open up about his experiences so you can discuss it and help put his mind at ease. Or you can simply give him time and space and let him realize just how amazing you are, and what he's missing out on if he doesn't commit.

But if not's his emotional baggage holding him back, and you think he's not willing to commit because he's intent on playing the field, then it's up to you to make a decision. Dating coach Suzanne Oshima says there is one thing you should do and one thing you definitely shouldn't. Do let him know that you are too good to be hanging on waiting for him to commit. You could even tell him you're keeping your options open so he'll realize he has competition! Yet she also says that the last thing you should ever do is give him an ultimatum. This will only push him away and it will not end how you want it to.

The bottom line is that the ball is in your court when it comes to how long you want to wait, but if it doesn't look like he's willing to commit and reach the step of calling you his girlfriend, then don't be led on to believe that someday he might. Let him go and save yourself the heartache.

11. He's different around his friends. He's super-sweet when he's texting you and comes across as the quintessential nice guy. But the second you're in a group setting and he's around his friends, he suddenly transforms into a rude, arrogant person you barely recognize. You'll probably be thinking your mind is playing tricks on you and that he can't possibly be the same person who stayed up until one in the morning texting you pictures of kittens.

Behaviour like this tells you one thing, he's horribly insecure and is desperate to come across as macho in front of his friends. Sadly, for guys, the quickest way to do this is to act like a cocky jerk, make lewd jokes and put other people down to make himself feel like a big man. So it's no surprise that you're probably wondering who the real him is.

Oshima suggests confronting him about his behavior and if he doesn't quit with the vain, macho facade then he won't be holding your interest. You need to make it clear that if he wants to be with you, he needs to be nice all the time, not just when it suits him.

None of these experiences are pleasant ones, but it's better to understand them so you can recognize them happening to you. Know the signs of a player and you can protect yourself from whatever tactic he throws at you.

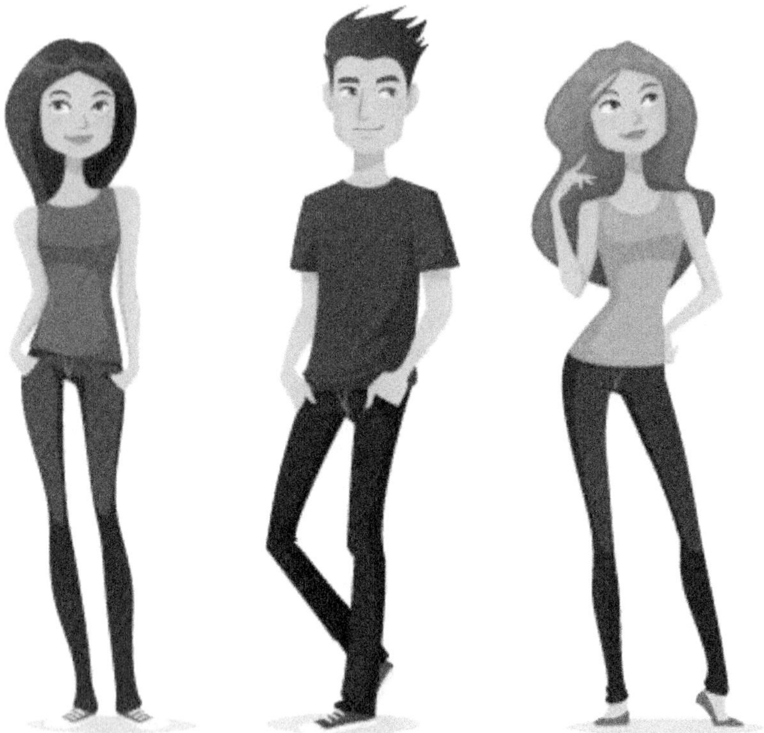

What to do if he's losing interest.

Maybe he's not playing games, but you notice there's definitely a shift in your relationship. Are you worried that you're drifting apart? Does it seem as though he's distracted and not making you a priority anymore? Maybe he's pulling away and you're worried he's losing interest. But what can you do to get it back? Here, we'll take a look at 8 ways you can win back his attention without coming across as needy and desperate. All it takes is a little time, and a little patience.

1. **Take a step back.** Giving him space might be the last thing you want to do, but it could be the most effective way to get his attention. If you notice he's texting you less and less, then play him at his own game and put your phone to the side for a while.

An easy way to do this is to mirror his behaviour. So, if he's ignoring your texts, ignore him right back. This works like a charm because without your attention, he'll be left to his own thoughts and company and he'll start to notice the hole where you used to be.

2. **Think about yourself.** It's no surprise that women take a knock to their self-esteem when a guy starts to mess them around and ignore them. In a situation like this, you have to

prioritize yourself and your mental health. If he's not giving you the attention he used to, then you'll have to give it to yourself. A lot of women confuse self-care for being selfish and self-indulgent, but that simply isn't true.

If he doesn't want to make time for you then make time for yourself. Text other people, spend time outdoors and do things that make you happy. Your self-confidence will grow and beam right out of you until he simply won't be able to ignore you anymore.

3. **Go out in a group.** If it feels as though he's pulling away, then suggesting you go on a romantic date with just the two of you might push him away even more. Especially if he doesn't want to be stifled by your personal attention. Inviting him out with a group of friends, however, will make things light and fun. And he will find the situation especially laid back if some of his friends are going to be there too.

What's so good about inviting him out in a group is that once he sees you having fun, and not just with him, he'll realize how much you don't need him to have a good time. He'll see you as a sociable person with your own wide circle of friends and that you're not sitting around waiting for him all day.

4. **Dish out the compliments.** We covered this earlier when planning how to get his attention, but

this time, we're paying him compliments to keep it. This has a two-pronged approach and works a little differently than before when you were just trying to get him to realize how attracted you were to him. First, if the reason behind him pulling away from you is based on stressful circumstances in his life, then texting him a compliment is likely to give him to the boost he needs. A text out the blue telling him how much you miss his strong arms or that he looked great the last time you saw him, will remind him how much you like him and could be the spark that reignites your relationship.

Second, maybe his interest was waning because he thought *you* had lost interest in him. Perhaps you were distracted, busy, or caught up with too many things in your life to realize you had been falling away from him. If that's the case, paying him a compliment will show that you still care about him and still find him as attractive as you always did.

5. Send a sexy selfie. Done right, this will absolutely send the sparks flying between you once again. Sending him a selfie of you all dolled up and looking your best will certainly grab his attention. Go a step further and make sure the picture was taken on a night out without him and he'll be extra desperate to see you. Now, it's more likely the tables have turned and he'll be chasing after *you*!

6. Stop putting him on a pedestal. When you're really into someone, it's so easy to think of them as the only person in the world you could ever be attracted to. I'll be honest in that I've thought just that way over girls before. Some people can just walk into your life and it's suddenly like they're the only person you've ever laid eyes on. But that's why it hurts so much when it feels as though they're losing interest in you.

The first thing you have to do is take him right down off that pedestal. You can do this by realizing that when you're overwhelmed by lust and attraction, your body is processing a bunch of crazy chemical reactions. These are making you see your crush, not as a regular person, but as someone who is so much better than yourself.

Consequently, this has a huge effect on your behaviour, and you may find yourself acting in a way that is more likely to send him running rather than make him attracted to you. When you obsess over a guy, you'll come across as desperate and clingy and that's just going to make him recoil.

Regain his interest by letting all those crazy, lust-based emotions run their course so that you are seeing him as a regular guy and soon enough, the obsession that was burning you from the inside out will dissipate. In turn, you'll come across as less desperate, more confident and therefore more attractive.

7. Let him know others are interested. I'm not suggesting you suddenly pick up some random guy just to make him jealous. That could go two ways. It'll either make him so upset he won't speak to you again, or he won't be fussed and will leave you alone forever. You can't risk either of those scenarios. What you can do, however, is let him know that he's not the only one texting you and that you have a life without him.

8. Get proactive. Maybe you're misinterpreting his disinterest as him just being too shy to make all the moves. If that's the case, it'll be up to you to get proactive and ask him out. Get him to travel to interesting places and make sure you spend time together doing fun things you both enjoy.

It's all about keeping up the momentum of seeing each other regularly and building up the excitement. Just make sure you don't pressure him to spend too much time with you. It's healthy to have time apart and any more than 3 dates a week could become a little overbearing for him.

9. Get him on his own. We talked earlier about spending time in groups, but on the flip side, do you find that he *only* wants to spend time with you when you're in a group of friends? Are you starting to think he doesn't actually want to be alone with you? If that's the case, arrange to have an evening with just the two of you.

You might find that it might not be a lack of interest that means he doesn't want to see you alone, but rather his own nerves and fear around getting personal with you. Put his mind at ease and let him know you don't bite.

These techniques should help you bring him back into your orbit in no time, but you should also remember that your sense of worth shouldn't revolve around him. If, after using all these tricks, he still appears disinterested, maybe it's time to call it quits. Let's move on to the next section where we talk about how you can do that.

Is it ever okay to break up through text?

The jury's out when it comes to breaking things off through text. Some people think it's highly rude and impersonal while others think it's normal. It's up to you if you think it's right or wrong to let someone go with a text message. For some people, it might depend on the situation, the person, the time, and your personality.

Breaking up through text is most likely to be acceptable when it's someone you've not known for too long. You wouldn't dump your husband of 5 years with a text, but it wouldn't seem wholly inappropriate with a casual hook-up of 5 weeks. But how do you do this? Don't panic because we've got 4 examples of texts you can send if you're lost for words, but eager to break things off.

4 Texts to Break It Off

1. *I'm sorry, but I just prefer you as a friend.* There is no shame in seeing someone more as a friend than as a romantic partner. Sometimes you just love spending time with someone and you connect deeply, but not in a way that's even remotely romantic or sexual. If that's the case, the sooner you tell them the better. If they value you and respect your decisions, they'll understand, and if they don't, and start complaining about

being friend zoned, then you're doing yourself a favor by getting them out your life.

2. ***I need to be alone to focus on myself.*** Some women are almost afraid to look after themselves for fear of appearing selfish. But what they have to realize is that you can't care for other people or meet your commitments if you're burned out and not taking proper care for yourself. Ever heard of the phrase you can't pour from an empty cup?

If you're finding that your new relationship is a drain, or that you need some time out for yourself, don't be afraid to tell him. If he truly cares about your health and wellbeing, he'll understand and give you the distance and support you need.

3. ***There's no spark.*** If, after a few dates, you're still waiting to feel some sort of connection to a guy, then you might start to feel that there's simply nothing there. This isn't anybody's fault, and you shouldn't feel guilty for not having feelings for him. However, you do have to be honest not just with yourself, but with him as well. Tell him as soon as you can so he's not hanging on thinking there's something happening between you when there's nothing at all.

4. **I'm not ready to date.** Maybe you've just suffered a break-up and wanted to get yourself

back out there. But now you've dipped your toe into the dating pool you're regretting your decision and you've come to the realization that you're just not ready. If this is what you're feeling, tell him you're just not able to make a commitment right now. Don't feel guilty or that you're letting him down, if you are not emotionally ready to date, don't feel pressured into it.

Let him down gently and explain that it's nothing to do with him, but that you're simply not in the right mental position to date him. He should have no reason to argue with you.

Good Luck!

I realy hope these tips have been helpful to you. Texting a guy and maintaining a relationship with him can seem overwhelming and exhausting at times, but with a little help and guidance it doesn't have to be. It can be as simple as following a few steps. Own your confidence, let him know how amazing you are. You'll be able to have the relationship you really want and be the queen of your screen, and have the man of your dreams.

Your Opinion is Important to Me

If you enjoyed this book and found some benefit in reading this, I'd like to hear from you and hope that you could take some time to post a review on Amazon. Your feedback really makes a difference to me.

If you'd like to leave a review all you need to do is to go to the book's product page on Amazon and click on "Write a Customer Review"

I wish you all the best for your journey!

Joshua

About the Author

Joshua has always loved language, and enjoyed every second of his English Literature degree, but he always knew he wanted something more. Always having a deep fascination with psychology and relationships, he began to wonder if he could use his talent with words to make magic happen between people. This took him on a journey to train as a relationship counselor where he could put his skills to use.

Now, Joshua still loves to provide couples with the help they need to succeed, but he still remains eager to teach people the power of words and communication. This has led him on a journey to discover how modern methods of communication can influence not just our modern lives, but our romantic relationships too.

Since then, Joshua has authored numerous books on communication, language, and relationships with a specific focus on kindling romance and setting that spark alight. His latest book, a comprehensive guide on how to text men has really let Joshua put his love for words and relationships into practice, teaching us the true power of texting in relationships.

When he's not working, Joshua loves to spend time outdoors with his dogs and reading a good thriller

Learn more about Joshua Bell here: *https://www.amazon.com/author/belljoshua*

Printed in Great Britain
by Amazon